LET'S LOOK AT
Pets

Nicola Tuxworth

LORENZ BOOKS

Dog

A dog has a furry coat and a wagging tail.

small, playful dogs

shaggy, long-haired dog

big, strong dog

silky, short-haired dog

Here are some of the things a dog needs.

brush

collar and leashes

bowl of water

biscuits

canned dog food

Baby dogs are called puppies.

Cat

A cat has soft fur and sharp claws.

gray, striped cat

long-haired fluffy cat

tortoiseshell cat

tabby cat

What does a cat eat and drink?

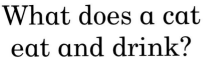

cat treats

dish of water

cat-flap

bowl of cat food

Baby cats are called kittens.

Fish

A fish has
fins that help
it to swim.

striped
angelfish

tropical fish

shiny
goldfish

dazzling
fish

fish tank

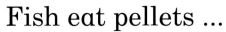

Fish eat pellets ...

... and flakes.

Baby fish are called fry.

Hamster

A hamster has a round, furry body and a short, stubby tail.

golden hamster

sleek pearl hamster

plump, brown hamster

Hamsters have pouches in their cheeks to store food.

Hamsters like to chew on lots of different things.

toys to gnaw on

dried food

seed stick

hamster cage

peanuts

Baby hamsters cannot see when they are born!

Rabbit

A rabbit has long ears and short, strong legs.

lop-eared
rabbit

brown rabbit

big, long-haired rabbit

What different types of
rabbit have you seen?

A rabbit eats fresh
and dried foods.

crunchy
carrots

dried
food

rabbit hutch

cabbage leaves

Baby rabbits
grow up in a
few weeks.

Horse

A horse has hard hooves and a long, swishing tail.

A pony is a small horse.

dappled, gray horse

bay horse

Have you ever sat on a horse or pony?

A horse needs lots
of different things.

grooming
brushes

water bucket

hay net

dried food

A baby horse
is called a foal.

Guinea pig

Guinea pigs have sharp claws and bright eyes.

gray and white guinea pig

long-haired guinea pig

tufted guinea pig

How many legs does a guinea pig have?

straw bedding

What does a guinea pig like to eat?

dried food

juicy apple

crisp lettuce

Baby guinea pigs cuddle up to their mother.

Pet playtime

You can play with a pet in lots of different ways.

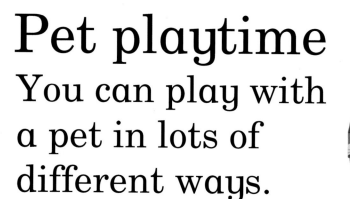

Stroke a rabbit gently to make friends.

Cuddle a guinea pig after you play with it.

It is fun to ride a horse or pony.

Cats purr
when they
are happy.

A dog likes to play
with its toys ...

... before going
to sleep.

Shhh!

Taking care of a pet

A pet needs lots of love and care.

A cat needs to be fed twice a day.

A dog needs lots of walks.

A fish tank needs to be kept clean.

Different pets need different foods.

Puppies are always hungry!

You should groom a dog with a stiff brush ...

... and a hamster with a soft toothbrush!

Which pets can you see?
What things do they need?